The Family Man's
Stock Market
Volatility Survival Guide

The Family Man's
Stock Market
Volatility Survival Guide

How to Defend Your Family in Any Economy

DONALD F. CARPENTER JR.

THE FAMILY MAN'S STOCK MARKET VOLATILITY SURVIVAL GUIDE
HOW TO DEFEND YOUR FAMILY IN ANY ECONOMY

iUniverse books may be ordered through booksellers or by contacting:

iUniverse
1663 Liberty Drive
Bloomington, IN 47403
www.iuniverse.com
1-800-Authors (1-800-288-4677)

ISBN: 978-0-5955-2069-5 (sc)
ISBN: 978-0-5955-0889-1 (hc)
ISBN: 978-0-5956-2136-1 (e)

Print information available on the last page.

iUniverse rev. date: 03/31/2016

This book is dedicated to the most precious human
beings I have ever known:
Aubrey, Kenyon, Olivia, Harmony, and Charles.

A good woman is hard to find, and worth far more than diamonds. Her husband trusts her without reserve, and never has reason to regret it. —Proverbs 31:10-11

My wife Lynn brings this quote to life. In her this project has found new meaning. Thank God.

Contents

Preface

All right, men! Here's one for you—a small book dedicated to the Family Man investor.

The stock market is down from all-time highs, the economy is weak, and nobody seems to know what to do. Newspapers and major financial websites are confusing the issue, and the advice on TV is just ridiculous. I'm here to tell you there is a way past the confusion and the madness, and that the way is calm, determined, and sensible.

I know, you hate that. You're used to go-go days, boom-boom markets, and stocks that just go up and up. Well, brother, it's time to

come to your senses. You've got a life to live and a family to protect. And my job is to remind you how to do it. Why just a reminder? Because you already know what to do. You know intuitively, as does every other red-blooded American Family Man.

Why is that? Because if you were born in the United States of America, the rules of success are infused into your consciousness— and if you were born elsewhere but live here you have the good fortune of learning by osmosis. If you've ever read the Declaration of Independence, you know what I mean. In that document, you've got all the knowledge you'll ever need to be a successful investor. Just dust off that document and get to know what it meant to its author and the good men who signed it. Get to know what it ought to mean to you. Remember, too, that every one of the men who signed it lost everything they had to defend the truths and principles written in it.

You might be saying, "Whoa, man ... you're getting a little political, aren't you?" I make no apology. This book does not pretend to be politically correct. And I'm sure a whole lot of people probably won't like that. Many of you may even be offended by title. That's okay. I promise you won't hurt my feelings. In fact, I wanted to title this book *Sticks and Stones May Break My Bones but Words Will Never Hurt Me*, but that was already taken.

So why did I write this book? Well I wrote it for my kids, their kids, and those yet to be born. I also wrote it for my extended family, my friends and acquaintances, because I know they're all a little worried about current economic conditions. I'm worried too. I'm worried that by the time this guide goes to print, the markets will have recovered, the subprime crises will be a distant memory, and stock market volatility will be anything but the mind-numbing bugaboo it was to the American investment psyche on January 22, 2008. I worry about that because, as we've all seen repeatedly, bull markets and prosperity, bear markets and poverty, tend to make people foolish, if not careless, if not just plain stupid—and that's a condition that can lead to a lack of preparation and lots of financial pain.

But sometimes pain is good, particularly the kind of pain that reminds you not to touch the hot stove again and again and again. Another good kind of pain is the achy muscle pain you get after a good workout. That kind of pain is a useful reminder that you're making progress. So if you've been hurt in these volatile markets, try to remember—after you've finished cussing out your stockbroker—that your painful experience will pass and that you can learn a thing or two from it.

Down markets are truly the greatest investment teachers. Often they remind us to refocus our attention on things that really matter, on our real priorities. In this book, the first priority of a Family Man is his family. The Family Man's family is the reason he works, insures, saves, invests, and then works some more.

Unfortunately, there are more experts than I can count leading you away from wisdom, prudence, patience, knowledge, and the practices of sound judgment. But, men, those days of being led astray into the desolate land of pie-in-the-sky are gone. You want wisdom—you need wisdom—and qualified or not I'm going to give you all the wisdom I've ever learned, from way too many years in graduate school and from my usual school of attendance— the Academy of Hard Knocks. Trust me, my blazer buttons even read *Collegeum Pulsationum Durarum* (The College of Hard Knocks), and proudly I'm still attending. You see, I learned every one of the solutions in this book the hard way—through trial and error—but the upside of trial and error is trial and solution. Thomas Edison once said "I have not failed 10,000 times—I've successfully found 10,000 ways that will not work". My hope is that you'll be able to steer clear of the same investing mistakes committed by every generation—due to fear and greed—and put my hard-knocks solutions to work for the benefit of you and your family.

Now is the time to redouble your efforts, pick yourself up from  the dust cloud of confusion, and bring patience, discipline, and American ingenuity back to your family. You can do it, brother!

Let's get started men! Onward to knowledge! We've got some work to do, so let's get to it!

Introduction

For Family Men Only!

The Family Man's Stock Market Volatility Survival Guide was not written for everyone. I'm sure anyone can glean important market strategies from it, but it was written for Family Men *only*.

Family Men, as you might have guessed, are men with families—families that they love, adore, and sacrifice for. So, if you have a wife and kids but you hate their guts, stop reading. If you're single with no kids, stop reading. If you're a player, a hoochie, a cougar, a badger, an international playboy, or a party girl—STOP—this is not written for you, and I guarantee you won't like what it says.

I'll make one exception, if you're a woman who's married to a Family Man or planning on starting a family with a man one day, thereby making him a Family Man, then go ahead and read this— you probably will like it. But I'm drawing the line right there! And I'm still calling this *The Family Man's Stock Market Volatility Survival Guide*!

To everyone else, *It's not for you*!

If you read this book all the way to the end, you will learn the following:

> How you became worried about your finances in the first place
> How and why Family Men ought to invest
> The 8 steps to protecting family wealth
> How to survive stock market volatility
> How and why American business survives in tough times
> Where money really comes from
> The 6 simple criteria for choosing an investment pro

"Hey wait a minute!" you're saying. "I thought you said this guide was about investing!" Well it is. But first you need to figure out *why* you're investing. If you're looking to outsmart the markets and cash in big on the next big mover, then please put down this survival guide and slowly back away. The Self-Help section is just two aisles over, and the Fantasy section is in another store entirely. But if you read this guide, you just might survive the insane market volatility we're seeing these days. You'll certainly straighten out your priorities when it comes to investing for you and your family—and buddy, when you're a Family Man, investing is always till death do us part. It's all about your family.

Are Family Men Too Scared?

There are many confused Family Men out there right now wondering where to turn and, worse, where the next shoe will drop. They're running around like desperate souls, searching for one last informative morsel of sustenance. I talk to them every day. Is the market going up? Is it going down? The only honest answer to these questions of volatility is an unequivocal and resounding yes! I'm sorry, but the stock markets will be going up, and they will be going down. If you haven't learned to use stock market volatility to your advantage because you're chasing performance and/or running scared, read on brother!

Are we in a recession? Are we headed for a depression? These questions are asked in wide-eyed bewilderment. Worried Family Men everywhere have their bewildered wide eyes glued to their TV sets, their thumbs glued to their Smart Phones, and their fingers glued to their keyboards in the ridiculous belief that, somehow, through all this strategic gluing, they're "managing" their portfolios and are going to "execute" their trades at a moment's notice. But they're just gumming up the family's financial works!

If you're using your Smart Phone or your TV to get up-to-the-minute market information, you'd be better off trying to catch machinegun fire with your teeth. Why? Because you're so far behind any event-driven move in the markets that you don't stand a chance. If you're going to attempt to manage your own portfolio, you need to be ahead of the curve, not behind it, and that means you need strategies to grow and preserve your wealth for years to come. Nervous Family Men are furiously scanning the daily financial press for any piece of encouraging news. Or worse, they've given up completely on the markets and are hiding in a fallout shelter in an undisclosed location with a sawed-off shotgun, a bottle of cheap bourbon, and a small pile of cash.

Our trusted and usually faithful guides in media appear to be shaken, confused, and disillusioned. Even the Federal Reserve Bank, the U.S. Department of the Treasury, the Congress, and the President seem to have been caught flatfooted. Questions of crisis and survival are taking on new validity as jobs are lost, personal and commercial credit schemes are increasingly taking over productive income streams, and citizens are waiting and wondering how high food and gasoline prices will go.

Take It Like A Man!

You called timeout for that little scratch? You call that an injury? C'mon buddy, shake it off! A little blood won't hurt you! Rub some dirt on it! You'll live! And I'm here to tell you you'll survive. This survival guide is written just for you, the Family Man, so you and your family can survive both current and future stock market volatility with purpose, confidence, and your dignity intact.

As Family Men, you've got a job to do, especially as Family Men confronting a scary-looking potential crisis. Why is it worse for the Family Man than for anyone else? Because Family Men have taken on the responsibility of supporting, sustaining, and protecting the lives of others. I know quite a few Family Men who feel they've taken it on the chin, and have the weight of the planet on their shoulders. As Family Men we've got mouths to feed—the baby needs diapers, the wife needs a new pair of shoes (yes, that does make it the ninety-ninth pair), the Cadillac needs a tune up, and guess what, you just maxed out the platinum card on a Pebble Beach golf trip for your buddy's birthday bash. Oh, trust me, it gets better! Read on Men!

How Did Men Get Here?

Okay, Family Man, let's have an open and honest conversation about priorities. You see the economy in trouble, right? You see that the global stock markets have swooned a bit more than makes you comfortable, right? In fact you're really worried. You're worried about a recession, about layoffs, about bills, about quite possibly the future of your entire family—retirement planning, college tuitions, little Debbie's wedding fund, food on the table, and gas in the Winnebago—right?

So how did it get so bad so fast? Weren't we just in the boom-boom days of a roaring stock market? Wasn't everybody and her brother buying up real estate like it was a going-out-of-business sale? (Which is funny, since that's what ultimately happened, isn't it?) So why were you so woefully unprepared for this downturn? There are

a lot of answers to that question, and frankly a lot of ways that question could be asked, but I think the most salient proposition I'm going to make in this survival guide is a two-part equation: you got yourself into trouble when you stopped taking your responsibilities seriously, and you can get yourself *out of* trouble with some determination and hard work.

We've seen a tectonic shift in the behavior of men in direct correlation to the acquisition of wealth. The wealthier we've gotten, the more careless we've acted. Not all men mind you, but certainly the men who have found themselves financially unprepared for market volatility and our current economic downturn. We started getting careless years ago. Admit it. Come on, look me in the eye. Wasn't that you trying to cheat reality, refusing to save, cashing out more home equity, clamoring for one more trinket? It *was* you, wasn't it?

I think a good place to look for some answers to the crisis men are in is something women have been noticing and lamenting for a while now.

Women!

Let's start our stock market volatility survival guide written exclusively for Family Men with a look at what women are saying about us. Why? Because we can't live without them, and when they're complaining about us, they're usually telling the truth.

"Where have all the good men gone?" they ask. That's a curious question. But it reveals a common disappointment among American women from east to west. The answer has a lot to do with how men, Family Men or otherwise, have changed in a culture of wealth and how those changes have affected the way men deal with their money.

Women are noticing that we men have made ourselves little—a little lazy, and a little too soft. We've become a little spoiled and a little fat—around the gut, between the ears, and certainly in the heart of our ambitions. "I want a man to sweep me off my feet," or "He doesn't challenge me anymore," or "If you say you want to do whatever I want to do one more time, I'll scream!" Have you ever heard anything like this? If you have, and you just rolled your eyes and popped open another cold one, then you're right in the center of a storm (one that you cannot see), and you might just be starting to think that the cause of her frustration really is you. Hey, it could be that she's just nagging you again; if that's the case, a good attorney,

a few thousand dollars, and half of everything you thought was yours can permanently remove the complaints.

Don't get defensive, man! I'm on your side. But let me ask you this: who do you think you're really hurting when you have one more beer as you channel surf, take an extra hour at lunch, and play video games on the computer at work, and put off work you should be doing today?

Who are you really hurting when you're putting off the work you used to love, the work you built our fortune on, only to pass it off to overworked and underpaid subordinates so you can strut around like you're a fat-cat little Lord Fauntleroy?

As men in the United States of America, we have had so much prosperity for so long that we believe two very dangerous myths: one is that our standard of living just magically appeared, and the other is that the good times will last forever. We want everything easy and we want it now. Because we accept ease as a birthright, we work a little slower, accept fewer challenges, and settle for just a little less. "A little less what?" you ask. A little less accomplishment, a little less ambition, a little less defined set of dreams. And women don't like it one bit.

Boys Will Be Boys

As pampered men, we crave the appearances of the wealth that surrounds us, yet we do less and less to actually earn it. We have managed to infantilize ourselves, preferring to remain spoiled little boys than become adult men. And as little boys trapped in men's bodies, we shirk responsibility, procrastinate, loaf, and squander away our money and our lives. And what happens to us? Nothing much. We live in an opulent world where we can slack off, slide by, convinced that spending money is our way to eternal bliss and that making an easy buck is still ... well ... pretty easy. And it is our sacrifice of integrity, ambition, determination, creativity, and wisdom that I believe our women are complaining about.

As spoiled little boys, we try to bribe our way through life—a cute little smile here, a helpful gesture there while throwing money at every problem. We beg the world around us for acceptance. We beg women for approval. "Look at me, Mommy! Approve of me, Mommy! Love me, Mommy!" We manipulate and bribe women with lavish spending, as if draping assets on them somehow proves our masculinity, when in fact it doesn't even perpetuate the myth all that well. She sees right through you. And we leave her no choice: if she's honest, she may accept our gifts but reject the boy; if she's worse, she'll take you for everything you've got.

All the good men haven't disappeared; they have simply remained approval-craving, spoiled little boys. We've just gotten a little too carefree about serious issues, but as Family Men (or, more accurately, as Family Boys), we've still embraced the appearances of marriage, family life, and child rearing—even though we are woefully unprepared, terribly underfunded, without a clue about managing our personal finances, and completely without the prerequisite stock market survival discipline.

We act like little brats stamping our tantrum feet to buy our next shiny new toy. At worst, we're drunken little sailors with a twelve-hour pass and a wad of cash on a spending spree like there is no tomorrow. But there is tomorrow, and there always will be. And on those days we pay dearly for the hangovers and headaches we've created of our lives.

Ask yourself, Dad, what life lessons will your children learn as you recklessly spend when there's not a dime set aside in a college fund, there's not enough insurance protection for the family, and all your high-flying investments are in the toilet? What lessons are they learning from your steady withdrawal from adult responsibilities? Could it be the old proverb "shirtsleeves to shirtsleeves in three generations"? Could you be laying the foundation for the impoverished future of your entire family? You bet that's what's going on! Hit the brakes, Daddy-O! It's time to search your soul. It's time to harness your potential, your intelligent creativity, and safeguard the importance of long-term family survival.

Be a Man!

In the olden days of yore, and in many cultures today, children had to *earn* the right to become adults. As a boy, you went out on a dream quest deep into the wilderness, fasted for days, struggled to survive, and came back a man of vision and purpose. As a boy, you left your home to hunt a wild beast and came back a man with its fur, fangs, and claws—or you didn't come back at all. You entered a terrifying gauntlet of challenges to prove your fitness for adulthood. You worked slavishly for years as an apprentice. You burned the midnight oil in tedious years of study. And in each of these endeavors, you worked so hard you felt lucky to survive. In some ways you didn't survive. Through this process, you were transformed; you left childhood forever to become adult forever. In a symbolic and necessary death, your child-life ended and you emerged from your rite of passage fit to be a man. You permanently left the comforts of irresponsible dependency to embrace the responsibilities of sustaining others. You evolved from a *dependent* of society into a *provider* of society. And you were given tokens and symbols commemorating the apex of adulthood your metamorphosis had reached: feasts, tattoos, scars, crowns, swords and shields, robes, medallions, mortar boards, herds of cattle, money, scepters, rings, and diplomas.

In today's world of grade inflation, title inflation, everybody gets a feel-good trophy, and tattoos as decorative decals, most of us have no

clear rite of transition, no formal method of learning the strategies of turning cowardice to courage, weakness to strength, irresponsibility to responsibility, and infancy to adulthood. What does this have to do with investing? Good question! It has as much to do with investing as it has to do with life. I believe that when you reclaim your status as an adult provider within your family, and more broadly your indispensable role of provider within society, you and your family just might survive these volatile times.

Prepare For Anything

Family Men are worried because they are faced with the reality that if things do take a turn for the worse, they might not make it. Do you know who First Baron Robert Stephenson Smyth Baden-Powell was? Remember the old Boy Scout motto "Be prepared?" In the early 1900s, Baden-Powell gave the Scouts that motto. When asked, "Be prepared for what?" Baden-Powell replied, "Why, for any old thing."

Now there is a wise, very useful, and entirely ignored idea. Be prepared for any old thing. The problem is we're not. We're still living in the foggy intoxication of high-flying markets that seem never to come down, markets where anyone could make a buck. You could spend your cash with abandon and rack up credit card debt without a single care, because in that market you thought you could always make up any shortfall in a hurry. And while the possibility of dire economic or tragic market events may exist (likely exist…think Black Swan events), I am telling you things are different now. So get yourself prepared, because if you are worried, you're not prepared. For what? For anything!

Real Work Powwow

Now is the time to get your family together for one of those quaint little family powwows and let everyone know they've got to all chip in some real effort because the family has some real work to do. Fortunately, getting you and your family prepared is not that complicated, but truth be told, it might be a little uncomfortable for a little while. You'll actually have to put down the remote, take off the ear buds, stop texting, and look at each other long enough to see if you still remember each other's names. Oh yes, you will have to speak, and you will have to listen.

The discussion should center on this theme: in a crisis, everything changes and everyone pitches in. Your family may have to tighten up, cut back, and exercise restraint and frugality. You might even surprise yourselves with the bond you build when everyone in your family is working toward a common goal. That's just what happens when you need to reinvigorate yourselves in a crisis.

It's kind of like what happened when you realized your favorite Hawaiian-print swim trunks were making you look like the muffin-top man and you decided you needed to slim down and tone up. Sometimes you've got to cut back on the doughnuts and that greasy double cheeseburger you love so much, do a little extra gym work, eat a veggie or two, and make yourself a little uncomfortable. You might get a little achy, a little cranky, and it may mean adjusting your lifestyle somewhat, but what are we talking about here? Only the survival of your family through the ages—no pressure. Like any other basic skill set you need to acquire for survival in the modern world—mixed martial arts, golf, tennis, sailing, saving, and investing—it takes time and it takes discipline.

But my guess is you're a little more motivated now, because the nightly financial news has been scaring the living hell out of you. Read on, brother. The answers to your worries are just ahead.

What's Love Got to Do With It?

I'm not getting all mushy on you, but I've got to ask, you love your family, right? Well then, take care of them! Secure for them at least the Maslowian basics. You remember Psychology 101, Abraham Maslow and his hierarchy of needs, don't you? Food, water, shelter, and clothing. If you're lucky enough to be married to a supermodel, her water will have to come in a fancy plastic bottle and her clothing will be made by a fashionista whose name will forever remain unpronounceable. But hey, she's your girl. You picked her, now feed her. She probably won't eat much, so count yourself lucky. You'll save a fortune on groceries, but trust me, you'll make up for it in shoes.

If you happened to take Maslow at his word, by now your hottie trophy-wife may have stimulated you into fulfilling the fifth human physiological need, and now you and she may be raising one or two precious little offspring. Feed them and clothe them too!

Get Your Heart around Your Business.

You're making money, right? That's why you're reading this survival guide, to give you some idea of how to manage it in these crazy markets. Before you think you're going to be the next John D. Rockefeller or give Warren Buffet a run for his, you need to get your heart around your business. You need to remember who you're really working for. You're a Family Man, and that means you're working for your *family*—not your boss, not your company, not your friends, not your neighbors, and especially not the appearances you've been maxing out your credit cards every month to keep up.

You're working for love. That's right! L.O.V.E. If you're not, then I suggest you figure it out and get your priorities in order. Start immediately! Because the sweet love of your life, that beautiful woman you put the wedding ring on while stammering "I do," and those adorable little rug rats you're so proud of that no one else can stand because they're just sooo perfect, are the reasons you're working so darn hard. If you are not holding them tight to the center of your heart's protective love, you ought to be. You gave your word, you made commitments to them, so be a man and live up to them. Just face it men: it is your family you are working to sustain, protect, and adore. They are the reasons you brave the concrete jungles day after day, slaving in the pits, hammering rocks with a sledge. Their survival depends on you. They are the sole beneficiaries of all your daily hunting and gathering. So first things first: taking care of business is taking care of your family. They are your first priority. You owe it to them and they will love you and respect you for it. No really…they really truly do love you. Really. I know you don't deserve it, but that's just the way it is. They love you. Get used to it.

Buy a Ferrari

Pay yourself first. There's a cliché you've heard a thousand times. But what does it really mean? Here's what it means: now that you and your tribe are fed, watered, bathed, and sheltered, it's time to start

thinking about what to do with the rest of your money. The first thing you'll want to do is run out and grab two sets of titanium golf clubs— one for you and one for the wife—a new F430 Spider red with egg shell interior, and that flame throwing $580K Cigarette boat!

Right? Not so fast, sparky. You've got a few more things to check on before you hop back on the drunk-on-luxuries train. One of the first things you absolutely must do is to make sure you C.Y.A. That's right! Cover Your Assets! You need an iron-clad, rock-solid, bullet-proof insurance strategy that ensures you never put your family in a

position to lose those basic necessities of life. Now it is time to protect yourself, your dearly beloved, and the toddlers.

For that you'll need a worst-case scenario plan, but we'll get to that in a second. For now let's just say you understand the basics—you get it, you got it, and you're smart enough not to lose it, because it is one thing for you to miss a meal or two while you're out hunting for the daily bread, but it's quite another for your four-year-old twins, Billy and Becky, to go to bed hungry because Dad didn't develop a defense strategy.

Fast Cash! Oh Yeah!

If you live in the United States today, investing couldn't be any easier. But the first thing you need to know about investing is that it's not called "fast cash" for a reason. It's called investing. So resist the temptation to listen to Uncle Louie, who knows a guy, who knows another guy who made a killing on ALDKRP penny stock. It's called *investing* because it takes time to build up a nest egg big enough to live on by tapping into *only* the appreciation, interest, and dividends as you bounce a grandkid on one knee. But you can do it. Simply put, as long as you have income, take a little of it, even if it's only $10 a day (if you're richer, $100 a day, if you've got rock star money, $10,000 a day, and so on), and stow it away until you can send a mutual fund company enough to buy into a fund.

Yes, there is more to investing than that, but for now we're keeping it simple. And if you really are a rock star, you shouldn't be reading this guide anyway, unless you meet the Family Man criteria. You also ought to know that you should have better investment strategies than mutual funds and/or groupies can provide.

Everything on 22 Black

You would be amazed at how many wealthy Family Men still think of the stock market as their personal roulette wheel. Conversely, some guys think it is too risky, and some don't think of it at all. Guys! Knock it off! That's not what your family needs! If you want to gamble, get a sitter for the kids and fly the wife to Vegas, or pack up the G4, along with the wife, kids, and nanny, and fly to Monaco.

You get the idea. Your trip will be more fun, the drinks will be free, and the shows will be *very* tasteful. If you think stocks are too risky, then start thinking like Warren Buffet. If you're not thinking about the stock market at all, you're probably the only genius in the bunch.

The stock market should be thought of as a market where businesses are bought and sold. If you can start to think of it that way, you can develop a prudent, well-diversified plan to capitalize on price trends and capture dividends. The problem is that the most memorable speakers on behalf of the stock markets are always the loud-mouthed, lip-flapping hustlers. What is it about snake oil salesmen that makes Americans love them so much?

I'll get to specific strategies in a minute, because I have a lot to say about strategies. But for now, understand this: Family Men need to know that there are wise and prudent stock investments that are good for you and your family. You don't need one more minute with one more TV carnival huckster trying to weasel your hard-earned cash from your hands for their "special trading systems," "market secrets," or stock market "do-it-yourself kits."

Oh, So You Thought Money Markets Were Safe

You like higher interest rates on your cash, don't you? Great. Just don't go crazy. Because for every higher point of interest your money market account is getting, you're undoubtedly taking on less stable investments, which you probably still believe are "cash equivalents". How would you know? But that's the new rule in a subprime world. Go see the move The Big Short. You'll see what I mean.

So while you're getting in the habit of socking away cash in a money market account, just make sure it's a money market account without exposure to risky investments, such as junk bonds, derivatives, and the like. When you have enough in your sock to buy into another mutual fund, do so with just a third. Keep the other two thirds in the money market account and start the process all over again. Now you're building your savings account and your investment account at the same time. And your little dears won't even have to break out the nuclear science to help you with the math.

Wait a minute! Don't tell me you're hesitant. Did you think your stock market returns were a bottomless pit filled with shiny gold doubloons somewhere next to the leprechaun and the rainbow? The key, now that the dust under your thinking cap is starting to settle, is to accumulate savings at a reasonable return for a cash-like

investment, which in this environment is somewhere in the neighborhood of 1 to 2 percent. It's not a ridiculous return, but it's safe. And safety is what you're looking for!

Earthquakes, Tornados, Fires, Oh My!

Now, back to keeping little Jimmy genius in college should dear old Dad stub his toe and be out of work for six months. Remember that cash you've been socking away? Well that needs to cover at least twelve to eighteen months of living expenses, and a piece of it should be paying an insurance premium, just in case your toe stub goes badly and you don't make it. I know, it used to be six months of living expenses, but that was before the financial "disaster premium" became part of the mix.

You see when really bad things happen, such as natural disasters or giant skyscrapers collapsing unexpectedly due to enemy attacks, messing up the place you call home, or worse—it takes a long time for the local economy to recover. So now we just play it smarter and prepare for longer down time. Don't worry if you don't have your emergency fund all stacked up and your insurance plan isn't in place right now. Build them a little at a time, but build them as quickly as you can. God forbid you ever have to use it, but when and if your family needs it, you'll know you're doing everything in your power to keep them safe.

Surgical Chandeliers for Sale!

It's time to pay the rest of your bills! Yeehaw! "No money left," you say? Oops. Then somewhere you've gotten your cart in front of your ox, and that needs to be fixed immediately.

My suggestion? Radical surgery. Probably some sort of ectomy, whether it be an ego-ectomy, luxury-ectomy, pride-ectomy, fool-ectomy, or my favorite, the terminally frivolous gottahaveitnow-ectomy. When confronted with an emergency situation—if you have no money left, trust me, you're in one—you might be forced to take drastic measures:

take another job (or two)

sell a chandelier (or two)

buy cheaper beer

eat at home more (yes, actually cook your own food—sounds crazy but it's really not)

trade down for an economy car without payments

rent fewer movies (you might even have to make googly-eyes a bit more often...)

shop less so you don't have to parade your new and important rubbish in front of your phony friends

Or you can save money by doing all of the above. I don't know about you, but if you're not taking care of the basics, you need to let go of the luxuries, even the small ones, because propping up this phony-baloney life of yours with a bunch of useless fancy dust-collectors to show off to people who in reality only despise you, is going to completely destroy you, her, and the kids. Wait a minute, you don't think those phony friends despise you? Okay, start shopping at Wal-Mart and bragging about your new bargain jeans. You'll see what I mean in a hot second.

Thou Shalt Not Covet Thy Neighbors' Life

You and your woman have to team up. It's you and her against the world, baby! You need to recognize it's your wonderful life together, not the neighbors'. Live it as a team with an unbreakable loving bond. Live your life together in a way that the family you're protecting does not have to suffer because you had to have a shiny new Harley with silver-studded leather saddle bags and custom chrome, cable access to every NFL football game, and a $3000 Louis Vuitton clutch with matching leased Mercedes convertible (to take the toddlers to private daycare). It's your life together; build a fortress of it—together!

Gold Star Disclaimer: If you're already on target and you love your family, take care of your family, work, insure, save, invest, plan, and protect, you've got the family completely covered. Guess what? You don't have to listen to a darn thing I'm saying. You're probably not terrified in an economic downturn either. Congratulations! You get to skip to the next section and go right to the front of the line with your shiny Gold Star. *And* you can have all the cool luxury stuff you can afford. Why? Because you're way ahead of the game. Congratulations! Way to go man! But a lot of very good, very industrious, and very confused Family Men do need to listen. So *listen up*, gents!

Up To My Neck in the Big Reality Show

If you're living your dreams without the means, you need to catch up to reality before it catches up to you and buries you alive. Generally, that means you've got to stop spending like a wild banshee with her purse on fire. Oh my goodness! The neighbors/friends/relatives won't think you're tycoons anymore? Boo-freakin'-hoo! Don't get me wrong. Luxuries are wonderful. I love them. I like top-flight cuisine, sports cars, great golf resorts, and comfy leather dress shoes made in Italy, but like the rest of us, I had to learn the hard way. Luxuries need to come in the proper order and at the right time. Trust me, there is no fancy car, no pair of Prada pumps, no Gucci purse, no matching pair of diamond-encrusted tennis rackets, and no lifestyle of the rich and famous so necessary as to leave your family unprepared and unprotected.

There is no *thing* that will keep you happy, and nothing will compensate for the love, trust, and devotion of your precious family. What would they do without you? What would they do in the case of your accidental disappearance? What will you do if you've left yourself devastatingly unprepared for the day you don't want to or can no longer schlep to the coal mine because your aged feeble body just can't lift another lump that day? Has it really come the point where luxury living is more important than homemade, where pretending you're rich by living on the double-digit interest payments of platinum cards is more important than protecting the ones you love?

Singin' the Money Fizzle Blues

We all make mistakes, and occasionally we get a little distracted. Sometimes it only takes commercial number fifty-seven out of the last fifty-seven Mercedes Benz commercials to finally convince you that you really do need to teeter on the brink of financial ruin to guzzle more gas. But you've got to realize the sacred mission you are on buddy! It's not an impression you're trying to leave your family; it's a legacy. It's not the fizzling emotional rush of passing fads they'll remember; it's that you provided safety, security, and some measure of deeper intelligence and meaning to their lives—and you did it because you loved them so very much.

Truly, you can figure out a budget with all the math you learned by the fifth grade. But if you're trying to prove you're more of a man to your buddies at the gun club than you are to your baby darlings at home, you've got a serious conflict. All the elementary school arithmetic calculations in the world aren't going to save you then. Maybe if you focused on what really mattered—the love and protection of your family—maybe if you took seriously your duty of becoming your family's financial mercenary, you might just conjure the strength, courage, and determination to get that all-important job done. And their reciprocal love, affection, and appreciation for providing all that security might just give you the courage to save, invest, and protect rather than show off. Responsibility, love, and devotion only return more of the same to you, and that might just make you smart enough to work, plan, and get serious about life's real issues rather than waste so much time and money just to brag—unless of course you're bragging about little Suzie's newest round of straight As.

But wait! What if the kiddies resist? What if they just get ticked off because you're not funding the weekly shopping-spree adrenalin rush? Hey! You're the Lawgiver. Lay down the law! At some point, all addicts—shopping or otherwise—need to come out of their buy-now-pay-later feeding frenzy and get into rehab. Sometimes it's just going to be the crucible-fired blessings of tough love. You don't have to be a jerk about it. Keep talking it over, but you've got to stop sometime, and now's the time. Gentlemen, it is time to evolve from a little boy who wants his toys into a man who sustains the family he loves. Will the love of your wife and kids save your life? It just might. Man up, do the math, do the budget, and get your family's collective butt back on track!

Be Better

As we speak, the price of gas in some places has gone up to $4 a gallon. Because of that, every wannabe hip-hop star where I live in Los Angeles is taking advantage of the plummeting prices of gas-guzzling Hummers. I was getting gas just the other day and heard the blaring beat of unintelligible noise resembling music coming from a brand new black and chrome Hummer as it pulled up to the next pump. This car was loaded! It had low-profile racing tires, shiny new chrome rims (why this makes sense on an off-road paramilitary vehicle, I'll never know), leather interior, and a phenomenal sound system. A kid in his thirties, resembling a more mature version of a Backstreet Boy, hopped out, baggy pants flailing in the wind, baseball cap turned sideways. He looked at me, gave me the "I know, I'm cool" chin-lift greeting, and pumped in $10 worth of gas. (I know because I looked. Hey, I was curious.) With 2.5 gallons of gas at 6 miles per gallon, by my calculations, he'll impress the hell out of his friends as he gets only halfway to work tomorrow. Buddy, get a car you can actually afford to drive!

You know and I know that car didn't make him any better. Perhaps it made him look cool in some circles, and I'm sure his girlfriend thinks he rocks, but in reality it doesn't make him better.

Don't sacrifice your personal economy and your babies' futures for pretention. Be better. Don't sacrifice your family's financial safety for luxury of any kind if you don't have the basics covered, because you really can't afford it. Be better. Don't waste a minute on toys, fashion, style, and appearances that are unaffordable, credit wrecking, and obsolete in three months only to find yourself unfulfilled, jealous, resentful, guilty, and poor. Be better.

However, if you want that shiny new quasi-military off-road vehicle hogging up your driveway, fine. Just get it after you've gotten the basics secured. Be better.

Costa Rica Girls Night Out

You know how to plan. You plan every day. You get up at the same time every day. Your route to work is so precise you know how to get there in heavy traffic with just seconds to spare. You have figured out both yours and your boss's daily schedule and know through meticulous reconnaissance where she is when you need a break. And if you are the boss, you know where to hide where no one will find you, until your cell phone rings on the turn after a disappointing 46 on the front nine.

You know what I'm talking about. We scheme how we're going to get the last cup of morning coffee from the break room without having to make a fresh pot. And you know what? We never get caught. You've spent ample time planning your next fishing trip to Costa Rica, girls' night out in Beverly Hills, and the dream vacation

in St. Bart's. You know the best place to get your nails and toes done and where to get the best cheeseburger in town.

You're a master strategist. So let me guess, your financial planning is all complete? Your investment strategies are all mapped out and funded? No? Well good thing you're reading this survival guide.

Figure out what to do, when to do it, and how much it's going to cost. Just like all the reconnaissance you did to find your favorite links-style golf course, you've got to spend some time planning out your future goals and then turning them into objectives. Start with the dream statement, "If I could do anything I want, I would !" For example, "If I could do anything I want, I would golf twice a week after I retire." Start by working backwards from your dream.

For example: pretend you're a wise thirty-year-old who says, *If I could retire at age fifty and play golf twice a week, that would cost me $200 per week, so I would need $312,000 saved up for thirty years of golf. Let's see, I've got $10,000 now, so if I add $106.70 a week at 8 percent (if you can still find 8 percent) until I'm fifty, that would just about cover it. That would be my best-case scenario. But is seems expensive. Maybe I'll play* *once a month or find a cheaper course to play at. The once a month price? $36,000, saved for thirty years of golf. But if I decide I absolutely cannot live without golfing twice a week until I'm 80, then I'd better find a way to ensure that I have that $312,000 of golfing money.*

There are many ways to do that. Do that with every goal, step by step. Prioritize. It takes work. It will take plenty of compromise, but really, that's about it, guys. That's as hard as it gets. But the hardest part, as well you know, will be the sacrifice…and it's called sacrifice for a reason…because sacrifice is good. Actually sacrifice is better than good. As the origin of the word illustrates, sacri = holy and facere = to do, in other words to sacrifice for you lovely little honey-muffin and the kids is to do something that will entirely transform your life.

We love you. Our super dad!

The Judge Says You Lose ... Everything

When it comes to your property, the most important job a Family Man investor has is keeping the greedy hands of Uncle Sam off the family fortune and the even greedier hands of lawsuit-happy vultures looking for deep pockets.

Let me ask you a few questions.

Question 1: What happens to your business, the family home, and your stunning collection of Ferraris and antique golf clubs once you're not with us any longer?

You've got two basic choices: (1) ignore the problem and let the government wipe out your family, taking half of everything you've earned and dictating to your family, at their expense, how the rest will be divvied up, or (2) do some very intelligent estate protection strategizing.

Understand this; this process should not be called estate planning. It should be called *multigenerational family wealth preservation*. The important questions are, do you have a *will* and do you have a *trust*? Don't think that just because you can answer yes and there's a set of dusty documents in a deposit box somewhere that you're safe. Ask yourself the following questions:

When was the last time you had your will reviewed or updated?

Has there been a birth or a death in your family that would require a document revision?

Have you divorced? Did you remarry?

Are there more children or grandchildren to consider?

Has your business grown?

Have you acquired significantly more property?

Is there anyone who is going to need special care and assistance after your passing?

Is there a favorite charity you'd like to leave a lasting legacy?

Your answers to these and many other estate-planning questions could necessitate a couple of hours with your friendly estate planning attorney. Is there someone at the financial advisory firm you employ who really knows you, who has helped you organize your goals, dreams and aspirations, and who can guide you through the intricacies of risk management, asset protection, and advanced planning? Talk to them. Get your advisor and your estate planning attorney well acquainted. Bring up the question of life insurance with both, because there are some brilliant estate planning strategies that can benefit from the placement of well thought out, premium-financed life insurance policies. Your basic estate-planning goal as a Family Man investor is to leave your fortune with those you love, not in the greedy hands of Uncle Sam.

Question 2: What happens to your business, the family home, and your stunning collection of Ferraris and antique golf clubs if you or someone in your immediate family has a tragic accident, resulting in severe injury or death?

If your assets are not properly protected, that umbrella policy of yours is just going to be the first morsel served up in someone's (not yours) tasty lawsuit. After that, your entire estate will be up for the devouring.

Question 3: What happens to your business, your business succession plans, your retirement plan, and that dream of sailing off into the sunset with honey-muffin, if your business partner suddenly drops dead of a heart attack and your new business partners are now his two twenty-something twins, Timmy and Tommy?

There are literally hundreds, if not thousands, of potential disasters out there. Everybody's situation is different. But the key is to safeguard your family. If you've made it this far in this survival guide, the hard part is behind you. Be proud, be brave. You're "manning up." You're securing, sustaining, loving, and protecting. Whew! You're finally getting back on track.

Chapter 2

Philosophies, Beliefs, and the Persistence of Markets

Family Men love motivational speakers! Why? Because we're saps. We love the movies *Rocky*, *Rudy*, *October Sky*, *Seabiscuit*, and *Cinderella Man* and cry like babies every time we watch them. They give us a sense that we can make it too—that we can make our dreams come to life. I'm here to tell you the same lessons apply to your family's financial life. You know that when you're motivated you do things, and when you persist at doing them, you achieve the thing you had imagined. You've done it all your life. You can do it with your family finances too, as long as you believe in American business.

Take a moment to read the following quotes:

"Whatever the mind of man can conceive and believe, it can achieve."

—Napoleon Hill

"Look at market fluctuations as your friend rather than your enemy, profit from the folly rather than participate in it."

—Warren Buffet

"There is no easy way to greatness in any venue, but if you work hard, good things will inevitably happen to you."

—Howie Long, Oakland Raiders linebacker

These three statements, by speakers from very different backgrounds and very different fields of endeavor, speak to the heart of the long-standing persistence of human achievement. And human achievement is at the heart of American business. The persistence of American business is most accurately represented in the charts of its major indexes—the Dow Jones Industrial Average and the S&P 500, to name two. The problem is that while most Americans work in American business, they seldom understand why it has worked so well for so long, and why the rest of the world is desperately trying to imitate us. It is even rarer to find anyone who understands the foundations of American business and why they are a record of persistent success. As the Family Men of America we need to know! To knowledge, men!

Jefferson Declares What the Creator Endows:
Life and The Pursuit of Happiness

There are many reasons investors both professional and amateur buy high and sell low again and again, consistently ruining their personal, family, and institutional fortunes. One of the worst is because investors have little understanding of, and therefore little faith in, the fundamental financial philosophy of our people. In general, investors do not believe that our market's time-tested, culture-based performance will persist. How they can still disbelieve after more than two hundred years of empirical evidence to the contrary, I'll never know. But it is a consistent and disastrous disbelief. Why? Because time and time again, it leads to portfolio destruction through one fatal behavior: panic selling.

Do not sell in a panic. Do not buy and do not sell for emotional reasons— PERIOD. Listen to Warren Buffet: *"For 240 years it's been a terrible mistake to bet against America and now is no time to start."*

Listen, men, the Declaration of Independence started the American stock market advance with Thomas Jefferson's declaration of our natural rights to Life, Liberty, and the Pursuit of Happiness. Natural rights, by definition, are rights you are born with. Jefferson's wonderful declaration is deeply ingrained into our national identity and tells us that we're free as American Family Men to work and to make money for ourselves and our families—we do not work just to give money to the church and we do not work just to give money to the state. We work for our Family! It is important to remember that this document is not mere poetry. The Declaration of Independence is the recognition and declaration of fundamental human rights. And those rights, so brilliantly described in that declaration, are inalienable. They cannot be taken from us. Remember, our government did not give us those rights. As human beings, we were born with them! The only job the government has is to protect our inalienable rights from tyranny.

The one inalienable human right fundamental to our pursuit of happiness—to our business successes—is the right to own private property. Thomas Jefferson and all the signers of the Declaration of

Independence were claiming as the foundation of human freedom the inalienable human right to own private property and the inherent right to apply human work to that property. According to Jefferson, these rights were granted to us by our creator, not King George or any other form of government. That being the case, we're motivated to work just a little harder, to pour our creative energy into our dreams, employ a few more of our brothers and sisters, build our financial security, and insure the safety of our families. You inherited a method of success that works, that produces real-world results, and a potential family fortress.

As Family Men of the United States of America, we must understand that as a culture, we've been in the business of successful business a very long time. There is a long-standing business tradition in our country, founded on American freedom and ingenuity, infused with persistence and discipline. American business success is often misunderstood and demonized, but it ought to be encouraged, preserved and protected, and handed down from each generation to the next. In the families where it is nourished and carefully gifted to our children and grandchildren, successes abound. Remember this, men, our success as a nation is not based on agreeing to any rights that Thomas Jefferson and our Founding Fathers *gave* us. They didn't give them to us. They declared the truth—these rights were *endowed by our Creator* and that we need to defend them at all times.

Believe in the Land of Cheap Traders

Some in the world see Americans as shallow, money hungry, and arrogant, yet others envy our systems of government and enterprise and do everything in their power to replicate them. Where Europeans are said to work to live, Americans are said to live to work. Our people have created industry as both a cultural ideal and a disciplined practice. While most Europeans receive nearly a full month off work for vacation, Americans are lucky if we get two weeks. If you own your own business, two weeks off may be unthinkable. If you're an entrepreneur, you likely live at work, wear week-old sweats, and live on delivered pizza, Chinese takeout, and Red Bull. From our industry we have created a land of prosperity, opportunity, and abundance.

I am reminded of a line from the movie *The Last Samurai*, in which Captain Algren drunkenly raised an obscene counteroffer to Mr. Omura, the emissary of the Emperor of Japan, for the training of the Japanese Imperial army. Insulted and frustrated, Omura's bodyguard said, "He's rude."

To which Omura replied, "That's how it is here [in America]. A land of cheap traders."

We may be considered a land of traders, and at times we may even be cheap, but I have stopped apologizing for American ingenuity and "know how", and its resultant prosperity long ago.

No Silly Utopias!

If we are anything, we are a land of successful entrepreneurs. Our culture is steeped in profit making—from paperboys to paper mills, from lemon-aid stands to soft drink conglomerates. We work to make money, to feed our families, to secure our lives. But you can't allow yourself to be lulled to sleep by your prosperity! And many of us are still blissfully snoring. Yes, evils and corruption exist in our nation. We've allowed that, because we've gotten too careless and too lazy. But if we are vigilant, those wrongs need not persist. And when there are rats in the barn, I say send in the terriers! We've got to be ever watchful and protective of ourselves, our families, and our nation. Come on, men! As caretakers of our society we've got to stay involved so our leaders, both in industry and in politics, don't try to pull another fast one. We've got to redouble our efforts to *keep them honest* and protect our rights.

I'm not propounding some silly utopian ideal. I'm describing a system of participation, created long before we got here, that still works wonderfully *if* we participate. Like every highly functional, highly productive system, ours depends on reason, free will, honesty, open communication, constant vigilance, in short—total involvement. And while we have spoiled ourselves to the point that many of our good Family Men teeter on the brink of consumptive infancy, as a people, we continue to be the world's most industrious and, as a consequence, the most generous. Our success in business has made us successful in philanthropy. Americans give more to charity than any other nation on the planet (look it up!). We are philanthropic because we can be, because we are very successful at our business endeavors, and because we know we ought to be. We are clever enough to make ourselves wealthy, and we're good enough to give some of those hard-sweat dollars to help others. Does that make us perfect? Not by a long shot, but I does make us pretty much the envy of the world.

If We Persist, Our Markets Persist

"What does this have to do with surviving stock market volatility?" you may ask. The point is this: as Americans, we are so successful at intelligent creativity, at making business work, and so driven to build successful businesses that there has never been a market correction from which our economy has not recovered. As long as we remain fundamentally business driven, profit motivated, and we keep our pay for our families (the definition of capitalist), our culture will continue to produce resilient economies that will raise the standards of living of all our people, directly and indirectly.

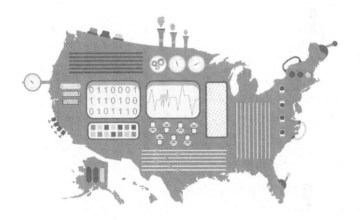

There have been market shocks, some severe to date, but we have recovered and markets have recovered toward upward-trending gains. A chart of the Dow Jones Industrial Average from its inception is not just an impersonal chart reflecting the profits of greedy corporations. Corporations are not evil machinations conjured in a nineteenth-century Charles Dickens novel, mystically designed by evil geniuses to destroy their employees and then the world. If you really believe that, then why do you keep buying so much of their stuff? Those all-too-common assertions are politically simplistic and just plain naive. Corporations are evolving organizations of human endeavor that at last glance still pay their human employees in the private property known as *money*. Those employees are still free to work at one corporation or another, if they so choose, and they continue to do so because they're rewarded with the private property called *money*. And with that money we feed our families, buy houses and minivans and health insurance, send our kids to college, get a flat screen TV or two, and buy a GPS device so we can make it back to work the next day.

Look in your medicine cabinet. Got anything from a store in there: Band-Aids, toothbrushes, shaving cream? Look in your garage, if you can get past all the boxes of stuff you're saving for who knows what. Got any motor oil, wrenches, power tools, a car or two? Look in the fridge. Got any milk, cheese, lettuce, or beer? Everything you see in your entire house, including the house itself, was built, grown, produced, and shipped for your individual convenience, directly to you, by a corporation. And why is any of this important? Because the Dow Jones Industrial Average or the S&P 500 doesn't represent the growth of the world's strongest inanimate, amoral automatons; it is a chart of human and cultural endeavor, a chart of our fundamental belief structures, and evidence of a fundamental aspect of the political and financial philosophies of our work—the ergosophic delineation of the American people. (My old college professors are going to be so proud of that line)

Let's look at an interesting hypothetical, a way for the Family Man to better utilize those indexes for accumulation of private property, which is by the way, the financial welfare of his family. If your family had enough saved to weather downturns in the economy—say, two or three years of living expenses in a worst-case scenario—and continued to invest new money during all the bear markets since 1929 (yes, I'm talking about a multigenerational family), your family would be wealthy generation after successive generation. How do I know?

Just follow the ascension of the chart. In the crash of 1929, the Dow fell to 230.07. Today the Dow is 12849.36. And guess what. We're being told daily it's the end of the world. Yet at every pause in the great American stock market ascension, we've always been told it's the end of the world. Listen to me, Family Men! With that simple investment plan, your family could have accumulated the resources to endow education, prosperity, and security to all its members, generation after generation, just the way the Founding Fathers would have wanted you to.

The Pudding of Proof Is on You

When I mentioned this idea to a dear friend of mine, who happens to be a great Family Man in his own right (and unfortunately a die-hard liberal), he shocked me with this response: "That's exactly what my Mom and Dad did for our family." He's a liberal, for God's sake! If his family could do it, every one should get a hall pass.

But you argue with my example and say, "Yes but not everyone had the means to save and invest in 1929."

"Good point," I say. "I don't care. Start now."

"Not everyone can save and invest now," You reply.

"Good point," I say. "I'm sorry for that. My family was dirt poor. My Mom, her brother and sister, and my grandparents all lived in a tiny ragged tent in depression-era Los Angeles. It happens. And unfortunately it happens much more than it should. What's at issue here, however, is not how unfair the world is but rather to get Family Men to understand how the world works, so they can make a difference for those in their care. In case you're not getting my point, this is not a "can't do" stock market volatility survival guide. What I am talking about—and who I am talking to—are hard working Family Men who run companies, own businesses, worked their way through the ranks, and struggled to build great lives for their families through their entrepreneurial endeavors and need good advice in volatile markets. I'm talking to rags-to-riches guys who thrill at hearing just one more hard-scrabble, hard-work success story and everyone else who sees the opportunities the work ethic of our culture can provide. I'm talking to anyone who has the drive to work long and hard, an inclination to philanthropy, and a desire to make a difference in their lives, in the lives of their family, and in the world around them. I'm talking to guys just like my grandfathers, who struggled through the Great Depression, fought in World War 2, and sustained their families through difficulties most of us can only imagine. I'm talking to guys like my Dad, who, without the benefit of a formal education but with determination and long years of hard work, made his family safe and secure.

If you believe in the persistence of our cultural identity—or at least the part of it that realizes that building profit-making businesses is an art, a science, and a phenomenon of human genius, all of which are reflected in the resiliency of our financial markets—as I do, then your family stands a good chance of being handsomely rewarded over time. Don't get me wrong. I'm not a narrow-minded flag-waving love-it-or-leave-it American; rather, I'm a keenly-focused equity-index chart and Declaration of Independence flag-waving American. At some point, my academic philosopher friends will point to numerous exceptions and will indeed disown me, but more than two hundred years of empirical market evidence is hard to argue. And I'm sure none of them will turn down their inalienable right to accumulate private property, represented in matching 401(k) contributions from their employers, anytime soon.

Even if we look at only the last sixty years, say from the end of World War II to the present, guess what. I still win the argument! Why? Because in January of 1946, the S&P 500 was at 18.02 and in January of 2015 the S&P 500 was 2072.36. You do the math! Family Men, it's time to believe in the American ability to build great businesses and make them profitable over the long haul for the benefit of the generations of your family and the freedom of our people. Just remember there were some serious corrections during those sixty years—so be prepared!

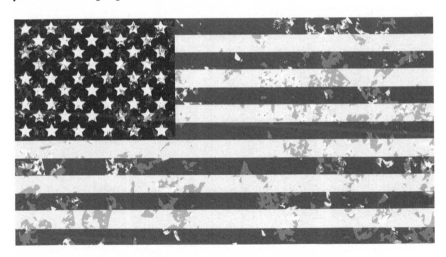

Chapter 3

The Sage and the Prude Are
Laughing All the Way to the Bank

In chapter 1, we covered why Family Men should invest, in chapter 2 we covered what American Family Men need to understand about the political and financial philosophies upon which our stock markets were built. Now we will examine the principles and practices of sage and prudent investing. Hold onto your hats gents! I guarantee it's not going to be what you thought. It's much, much better! Dare to be sagacious and prudent, and dare to teach your children sagacity and prudence, and your chances of creating substantial family wealth will be greatly enhanced.

This section has twelve major propositions (as well as several bonuses ones) to help you become a sage, prudent investor. Taken collectively, these sections will teach you to become a more informed investor, prepare for volatile markets and economic downturns, and develop strategies for success. We're in the home stretch, men, but we've got some work to do, so let's get to it!

1. Study Like a Man

Don't be a blockhead, a nincompoop, a numbskull, or a nitwit. I have to laugh every time I hear children say, "I'm not good at math." Oh really? I'll bet the first time you sat down in front of a piano keyboard you were riffing out variations on a theme of Mozart's "Eine Kleine Nachtmusik," weren't you? The good news is, your brain is like every other muscle in your body—the more you exercise it, the stronger it gets. The bad news is your brain is like every other muscle in your body—the more you sit it on the sofa in front of your television with two pounds of chips and a gallon of frosty soda, the lazier and consequently the stupider it gets.

Study like a man! Develop a regimen. Practice, practice, practice. Take responsibility for your financial knowledge. Make some time to read the _Wall Street Journal_, the _Investor's Business Daily_, and the _Financial Times_. Read books by and about the best investors, people like Benjamin Graham, Warren Buffet, and Peter Lynch. Build yourself a little library of good money books. Read articles posted to the Internet. There are thousands of them. Thanks to the internet, there is very little information that is not at your fingertips any more. But read with caution. Train yourself to be shrewd. Learn to distinguish between wisdom and silliness, between sound investment practices and ridiculous gambles. Learn to manage risk!

While you're at it, read books about history, the rise and fall of civilizations, and the rise and fall of companies. The two have a lot in common. Study economics. Learn how your government works, where all your tax dollars go, and why the Federal Reserve and the Treasury had to bail out Bear Stearns and GM. Learn the enormous difference between entrepreneurial capitalism and crony capitalism. It will help you. You don't have to become an expert, but you can become a student. After all, it is your survival and the survival of your family we're talking about. These things take time to learn, so remember patience. At least you'll be the hit of your next cocktail party (if you're not too smashed) and you'll be able to have an intelligent conversation with your investment advisor. And you can find out if he really knows what he says he knows.

2. Resist Idiot Box Confusion

Resist the television. I love the John Mayer song "Waiting on the World To Change," which contains the lyric *and when you trust your television what you get is what you got, 'cause when they own the information, oh they can bend it all they want.* The television is a great invention. It is the most effective sales tool ever invented. However, the Family Man must teach his family to view it with discretion or go ahead and unplug it altogether. He must teach them to examine things with the eye of a skeptic *before* they buy. The television will keep you in front of itself at all costs and is designed to keep you sitting in front of it just long enough to sell you all the fancy products on its commercials. Q: Why do you think most weather girls wear tight blouses? A: To make what is going on in the TV screen more interesting than what's actually going on outside. Wouldn't it be easier to go to the window and look? Or dare I say, to walk outside?

The other parts of the news operate in similar fashion. They present the facts in interesting ways, designed to make you linger long enough to be curious. The news wants to keep you in a constant state of anticipation. What's on next? Stay tuned! We'll be back in a minute with the rest of our fascinating story! Recently, however, the news has been downright hostile, particularly the financial news. (It's almost as if it's trying to influence an election. Do I sound cynical?) The financial news has not just kept you curious; it has kept you frantic and almost terrified. The market is going down! We're headed for the worst depression since 1929! It's the end of civilization! Martians are attacking! Lions! Tigers! Bears! Oh my!

The financial news has been at its all time worst. It is a demon worthy of exorcism. It is conflicted, destructive, schizophrenic, or all three. They're certain every downturn is the end of the world and every upturn is the beginning of nirvana (which coincidently enough is also the end of the world). The economy will never recover. Every new disaster is more devastating than the last. But on the other hand, pie-in-the-sky is the new world order. Life as we know it is just one big forever-frolicking party!

If you let the financial news hypnotize you into believing it can help you with your investments, as if it were the financial gospel, you will become part of a vast herd of believers. The herd buys when everyone else is buying, and the herd sells when everyone else is selling, and hot stocks are chased up the mountain, down the valley, and right off the cliff, trashing your best financial intentions. One thing is certain, if you watch TV for investment advice, you will have absolutely no idea how to manage your money.

Let me ask you an important question: Who do you think the counter parties are to all those blue chip sell transactions so frantically reported from the floor of the stock exchange during a major market correction? Who are the guys buying? Answer: it's not anybody that is taking the doom and gloom of the financial news seriously. And more importantly, it ought to be you, the Family Man investor buying the best companies in the world at rock bottom prices! Just manage the risk! You go, boy! So while the news is trying to scare the stuffing out of you with endless confusion about crashes, recessions, and depressions, you can do one of three things: steel yourself with real knowledge (book learnin'), turn the channel, or both.

Actually, the truth about investing for Family Men is simple. Here are eight easy steps:

1. Love your family.
2. Take care of your family.
3. Work.
4. Insure.
5. Save.
6. Invest.
7. Plan.
8. Protect.

Don't get me wrong, I love watching the financial news. I yell at it all the time. It keeps me fully stocked with a fresh supply of nonsense to laugh about with my friends.

3. Grow Corn in the Beneficent Universe

You've got to learn to grow corn in a beneficent universe. What the heck? No. I'm not talking about turning your corn flakes into ethanol, corn liquor, white lightening, or any other distilled byproduct. Just plain, old-fashioned corn. If you plant a kernel of corn and nurture it to maturity you, what do you get? A stalk of corn with about six to eight ears on it. And what is on each of those wonderfully sweet and plump ears of corn? No. Not a thimble full of ethanol. The answer is hundreds of kernels of corn. This will equal 7 hundreds of kernels of corn if you add up all the ears on the stock. And where did that stalk, all those ears, and all those kernels come from? One tiny little kernel of corn, well nurtured to maturity.

That's the way the universe works. You start with one. You work hard. You invest. You nurture your investments. Let compounding interest do the heavy lifting. And how long before you double your money? Use the Rule of 72 and find out. For example, if you invested $1 at 10 percent annual rate of return (not that it's easy to get 10 percent anymore), it would take you 7.2 years to get $2. If you invest a

$1 million at 10 percent, it will take you 7.2 years to reach $2 million. Divide 72 by your rate of return, in this case 10 percent, and that provides a rough estimate of how many years it will take to double your dough. Yeah!

4. Learn Where Money Comes From

Most spoiled children have no idea where money comes from, and neither do most spoiled adults. The fact is that money comes from WORK. In fact, if you want to save your money, preserve your money, and grow your money, all that you save, preserve, and grow will come from Work. Unless you're an heir to a big pile of cash, stocks, and bonds, most of your money will come from Work. And let's be truthful here, if you inherit all your money, it did come from someone's Work—just not yours. If you are that fortunate heir, *someone* will have to Work very hard to hold on to it for you. Here's the great disillusionment of many closet "high rollers": 80–90 percent of the money you live on after you stop Working will have come from money you earned *while Working*, NOT investment returns! And that, boys and girls, is the story of where money comes from. Money comes from Work—not market returns, not hoping and wishing, and rarely from the lottery or Las Vegas. So continue to Work. Add money to your investments every day. Work. Add money. Work. Add more money. Don't get cute. And so on...

5. Feed the Beautiful Beast

Are you still disillusioned? Come on, be a man. Suck it up! Did you think your Uncle Louie was telling you the truth when he told you he once knew a guy who knew a guy who knew a guy who made a killing in the market? Occasionally it happens. And occasionally someone gets wiped out in the market too. Those "killings" are the exceptions to the rule and cannot be duplicated (well, the making a killing part cannot be duplicated; the getting wiped out part is duplicated every day), and certainly the dreams and aspirations you hold dear for your family and yourself should not depend upon exceptions to any rules.

Those "killings" in the market are usually the product of dumb luck, lucky luck, hard working luck, genius luck, and any and all other iterations of luck. This means you're still going to have to work—unless you get lucky. While you're still trying to resuscitate your obsolete belief system about how rich the markets were going to make you, stop! You are a Family Man and have important work to do. You don't need pie in the sky.

With that in mind, I'd like also to mention the fact that while you're working at building your financial fortress, it is a beast that must eat. On regular intervals, just like nursing a baby, you need to fund your future dreams with extreme regularity. Be systematic, be disciplined, and don't get cute when the market runs up or down. Don't jump in and don't jump out. People who study investor behavior say, chances are the fear that drove you to the sidelines will keep you there when the markets turn around. Why? The human brain is just hard-wired that way. But you're working on building a tradition of multi-generational family wisdom here, so just feed your beautiful beast. Be consistent. Yes, there are some exceptions at the irrational extremes of human behavior regarding markets, but we'll talk about those later. For now, know that your little baby of a financial fortress will one day become a beautiful beast of a financial fortress, if you feed it every day, every week, and every month, year after every year. Feed it with gusto, because that beautiful beast will one day—if you're wise, prudent, and patient—protect you and your family for years and years to come.

6. Go to Asset Classes

Like my favorite former hedge fund manager says, If you're still using one of those 70/30 allocation models most firms are still using, you're "suffering your 3rd global equity implosion of the last 15 years…your being self-taught!" Family Men know the basic differences between asset classes, including how over concentrations in any class can affect your wealth over time. Learn to think of your investments in terms of class, not in terms of which individual stock will make you rich. *Stop* thinking about and wishing for hot stocks! Old habits die hard—I sympathize—but die they must! Learn how the various classes work together in the current economic cycle, how they should be allocated over time, and if you're a long-term investor, pay attention at least quarterly—not every day—to their value. But analyze that cycle carefully, and I think we should watch central bank planning decisions just as carefully. They matter! Check your portfolio value as often as you check your house value. And if the value goes down, for goodness' sake, please do not sell your house to the lowest bidder (just kidding!) We used to read the asset class study entitled *Determinants of Portfolio Performance*, by Brinson, Hood, and Beebower. "Why?", you ask. Because it revealed that 93.6 percent of portfolio returns are determined by *asset allocation*, not stock selection and not market timing. So many firms would say "it's *time* in the market, not *timing* the market." But the truth is, things have changed.

Funny the way the truth can inspire a crisis of faith—sometimes it is exactly the opposite of what you believed all along. Wait! What doesn't work? Exactly! So, stop thinking about and wishing for hot stocks or boom-boom markets. Stop it right now. Listen, you can believe whatever you want. You can be the Mr. Carlson of stock investing. Mr. Carlson, the owner of WKRP in Cincinnati (an ancient TV show), threw twenty live turkeys out of a helicopter as a Thanksgiving promotion for his radio station. He believed turkeys could fly. The sadly funny thing is, they can't. Here's the transcript from news anchor Les Nessman: *"Oh my God, Johnny, they're turkeys! Johnny, can you get this? Oh, they're plunging to the earth right in front of our eyes! One just went through the windshield of a parked car! Oh, the humanity! The turkeys are hitting the ground like sacks of wet cement! Not since the Hindenburg tragedy has there been anything like this!"* Turkeys can't fly, and hot stocks won't make you rich. But, of course, you're free to believe anything you'd like.

7. Diversify

Family Men never forget the hard and tragic lessons learned on someone else's watch about mismanaging money. So remember the hard lessons of the employees of Enron, WorldCom, and Bear Stearns: *Do not* keep all (or even most) of your eggs in one basket! Always diversify. Diversify across asset classes and diversify within asset classes. Diversify across investment styles and diversify within investment styles. If you're using mutual funds or ETFs, watch for overlap that can spoil your careful diversification strategies. For example, almost all blue chip growth funds have Microsoft in them. You could inadvertently be out of balance and heavy in Microsoft, even though you have several different funds. Yikes! Learn to manage risk! The affluent Family Man can afford to move beyond the use of mutual funds and on to the better pricing and tax structure of separately managed accounts, so make sure your managers aren't inadvertently creating position concentrations. You and your financial advisor need to be watching the managers at all times and coordinating their efforts.

There is no guarantee that diversification is going to make you one dollar richer or spare your portfolios from lagging in a downturn, but a study written in 2004 and published in *Forbes* magazine, entitled "How to Stay Rich," showed that a lack of diversification and huge stock concentrations were major factors in the loss of wealth. Stock concentrations didn't just make people poorer; they actually got them kicked off Forbes' list. Now that's gotta hurt! Diversification is smart, so make sure you do it.

8. Real Men Analyze Themselves

It is amazing how many seasoned investors are long term when markets are running up and instantly become short term when they are running down. Switching from short to long to short term based on market sentiment is not a strategy for success. This strategy, known by its more familiar name "panic selling," is a most destructive behavior and a leading cause of portfolio disasters. Analyze your tolerances for risk, and analyze them as they change over time. Know what risk is, what volatility is, how they differ, and how to respond to them. Analyze your risk tolerances when you get married. (Okay wait until you get back from the honeymoon.) Analyze them again at the birth of your first child and at the birth of your first grandchild, as they may have changed. Analyze your risk tolerances when you're about to retire—say, five years out—and Analyze them at the passing of a loved one. Family Men know that the markets are at best emotionally neutral and that it is their response to markets that they must control. It's easy to have a risk-tolerance evaluation done online, or ask your advisor for one. Take the results seriously, know how you'll act in a crisis situation, real or imagined, and then hold on tight. It's going to be a long, bumpy ride.

 ## 9. Balance and Rebalance while Cycling

Family Men know who's running the show. (So after you've checked with your wife…) make sure you don't let your outperforming stocks try to upstage her by trying to run the show. "But I like to cut my losses and let my leaders run." And I like to scuba dive in the shark infested waters off Catalina Island with fresh chicken livers tied to my butt. That doesn't mean it's a good idea. Asset classes are historically cyclical. So for goodness sake learn to recognize market cycles. Learn to see a growth cycle as it's developing and a recognize a cyclical slowdown before it happens. If you get too top heavy in one class, you may soon find yourself undiversified, out of balance, and suppressing your portfolio's efficiency. If you've had significant growth in any one class, rebalance your portfolio. At a minimum, you should rebalance your portfolio annually. A more analytical approach might be to rebalance your portfolio according to where the economy is trending in the business cycle. As growth grows and as growth slows, you'll need to adjust accordingly. Ask yourself this: "When is the best time to buy bonds and when is the best time to buy stocks in an economic cycle?" If you don't know, find out!! Since you're still accumulating wealth, spread your money across several asset classes. And from time to time, add a non-correlated asset class, something that performs irrespective of stock and bond markets. Perhaps a market-neutral hedge fund or a managed futures fund would fit the bill. Some seasoned analysts suggest accumulating physical .9999 gold coins and bars, say as much as ten percent of your investable assets. If you always let your leaders run, you just might have to remember the old Wall Street adage the hard way: "Bulls make money, bears make money, pigs get slaughtered."

(Disclaimer: The example of fresh chicken livers was for illustration purposes only. Do not try this at home. Neither fresh chickens nor their livers were harmed in the writing of this survival guide.)

10. Opportunism and Stock Mob Madness

Keep a little powder dry. By this I mean you should keep a cash reserve for opportunistic moments in the wild madness of a stock mob. When everybody in the stock mob has eaten their fill of locoweed and starts wildly stampeding toward the exits during the

enormously gigantic end-of-the-world stock sale (say a 20–40 percent market correction or better, like the one on January 22, 2008, or March 10, 2008 to name a couple, or any yet to come), allow yourself to buy those bargains at bargain prices, but do it while managing risk.

Conversely, when everybody in the stock mob has eaten their fill of locoweed and starts wildly stampeding toward the entrances, driving the markets higher and higher—and more importantly, when

professional analysts have joined the stock mob, proclaiming the old order dead and that euphoria will ever abound in the new utopia—sell your biggest movers. Learn how and when to take some money off the table. Learn to manage risk. You can never lose money taking profits, even if you're a bit early. It's hard to do. You've got to have ice in your veins, but you're a Family Man;

you have good reasons at home to do it. It really is best to stay clear of crazy lunatics and their irrational exuberance (or their catastrophic pessimism). You ought to be opportunistic and buy the biggest, strongest companies you can find when everyone else is giving them to you dirt cheap.

11. Women and Children First!

Remember, you're doing all this discipline, study, and work in defense of your family. And it's not just your wife and kids you're working for, although they are the most important, but your grandchildren, your yet-to-be-born great grandchildren, and the generations to come who will bear your name. If you're working with a legacy in mind, I believe you'll work harder and smarter, and when everyone else is panicking in a tough market, you'll know why you're still at it. Your investment disciplines and practices really are for purposes greater than yourself. More than money, you've got love, dedication, and commitment to contribute to your family, and your talents, wisdom, and strength are the significant attributes you will leave as a legacy.

There is an intelligence yearning in the heart of every Family Man to make a difference in the lives of his family. The important thing to remember is that you are making a difference now, and with hard work and discipline, you will make their lives even better.

12. Hire a Pro

This final section is so important I've decided to devote an entire chapter to it. So, without further ado...

Chapter 4

Hire a Pro

(When it comes to hiring an investment advisor I have some strong biases. The reason being, I've worked in the financial advisory industry for some 20 years and I've seen and heard some pretty "amazing" things. What does that mean? Simply, I've got a bone or two to pick. For starters, I've never really liked the salesman-masquerading-as-investment-guru approach of many advisors, and I truly loath their mimicry of the screaming heads on financial TV. It seems to me the best advice and maybe the rarest advice is to learn to manage risk. Having said that, read on Family Man!)

Once he has comprehended the enormity of the task, the intelligent Family Man might want to consider getting some well-qualified, competent help. The U.S. Bureau of Labor Statistics (BLS) expected the financial industry to grow at an annual rate of 1.2 percent between 2002 and 2012. That suggests 964,000 people entered the field, creating almost a million new jobs by the year 2012. Current estimates from the BLS expect a 9 percent rate of growth within the industry between 2012 and 2022 or an additional 394,000. With everybody and their brother jumping into (or since 2008 out of) the financial services industry, how does the prudent Family Man tell the difference between a knowledgeable professional, an innocent ignoramus, and the devil?

One of the best selection tools on the planet is located right between your ears. Again, you'll need to do some research, but you'll find it. When you do find it, fire up that bad boy brain of yours and put it to work! Finding someone to help you with your family's nest egg is important. It may be as important as finding the right doctor to care for your children. Why? Because it is caring for your children! Haven't given it much thought? Now's the time!

Do-It-Yourself Tinkering Is for Kids

Let's see, you've got a tennis pro, a personal trainer, a yoga instructor, and a different doctor for every part of your anatomy, but you're still using a stockbroker, or worse, you're managing your own investment accounts? Unless you're Michael Barry (he managed Scion Capital netting 489.34%) get with the program! If you're working on your own project/business/life/goals/family, you may be just a little preoccupied. And because you are well past the early years of your investment life cycle, you need to be sold another new investment idea like you need a new anvil tied to your leg. Those well-intended new ideas are slowing you down. They're mixing you up. You're being played. Someone once said the definition of insanity was doing the same thing over and over while expecting a different result. That's exactly what you're doing with your newest "investment idea." And unless you have another twelve to eighteen hours a day for analyzing, strategizing, and managing your own investment accounts, doing it yourself can be a very onerous task.

The best time to have started a do-it-yourself investment program was long before you had accumulated any assets, maybe even before you had gotten your first job. You were young then; you could weather storms of uncertain market volatility rather easily. Your peak earning years were way ahead of you. When you were working your first job, your opportunities to learn the basics of budgeting, insurance, mutual funds, and stock picking were at their greatest. At that point in your life, all that mattered about stock markets was learning about them—not making a killing. While your accounts were relatively small, you learned an important lesson: just how hard your investments were to manage, particularly in volatile markets.

Teach your kids to understand the financial markets as early as possible. If you don't know that much about investing (once you've studied and realized you really don't), a great family project would be to learn together. Just don't let your kids get it into their little skulls that gambling is their key to financial success, because their first market downturn is more likely to show them that the stock market is a waste of time, permanently undoing all your lessons to "invest wisely." But remember, Dad, after you've made a few hundreds of thousands of dollars, you should consider hiring a pro.

Everybody Is A Genius

A while back (2013) as I was walking down the hall of my office building, an attorney friend of mine stopped me and we had the following exchange:

"Hey what's going on with this market?" he asked in pitched frustration.

"Well," I responded, "it seems, according to several important indicators, that now may be a good time to buy some very reasonable bargains, because—"

I was just about to give my rational for investing at a market low, when he cut me off, his eyes narrowed. "No!" he said emphatically. "The news says we're in a recession, but the market is up today!"

I replied, "and if the stock markets continue to move up incrementally, the idea of a recession may be very short lived."

"No!" his said, his voice more pointed. "The stock market is all about speculation and only for speculators!"

To which I defensively replied, "Well that's one way to look at it, but it is the wrong way."

He snickered, narrowing his eyes again, and briskly walked away. I think we were still going to be friends. But his frustration belies the frustration of many a do-it-yourself investor in volatile markets. The fundamental failure of many do-it-yourselfers is that they do not grasp

this hard-learned idea: *managing stock investments isn't easy*; even for seasoned portfolio managers, it is a herculean task. It is so much easier to be a stock-picking genius when the market is running up. Isn't it?

So Many Advisors, So Little Time

I say start with the one who understands that the most important thing you own are your dreams and aspirations, and that the most important things you do are work and save and protect your family. This order of priority puts "investing" and by default financial "advice" in proper perspective. It's all about your family Mr. Family Man!!

As I said earlier, once you've decided to hire a pro, you'll need to do some homework and decide which type best suits you, the affluent Family Man. Today, the growing number and types of financial advisors are staggering. Even attorneys and accountants have jumped into the financial advice business. But whomever you choose, you need a modicum of competent guidance through the stages of prosperity—from investment ideas (at the very beginning) to proven wealth-management methodologies all the way through to legacy concerns. The latter two are the most complex, requiring qualified skill sets and legitimate strategies.

Although the field is growing, very few can perform all these tasks alone. In my opinion, most of the people working on the retail (customer-acquiring) side of the investment industry know either investment products or financial planning—and quite often little of both. The reason why is obvious: it's just much simpler to have a narrow field of specialization. As many have discovered the hard way, although many of the larger firms have changed the names of their account executives and stockbrokers to "advisor" and/or "consultant," these employees are very rarely rewarded for the useful knowledge they acquire for your benefit. Rather, they are rewarded most for the sales they make, the fees they generate, and the accounts they land. God forbid anybody should spend a second managing your risks, both personal and professional, protecting your assets (let's just start with the wife and kids), zeroing out your tax liabilities, and helping you build your rock-solid financial fortress.

It's So Easy a Monkey Could Do It

Let's face it, that's what drove you to try to manage your own accounts in the first place. You knew you could do better than your advisor and at a fraction of the cost. After all, you were both operating from the same knowledge base when it came to investments and management strategies—little and none. Typically advisors are salespeople and you're a businessman; neither of you have the skill set(s) and analytical team to manage interconnected complex markets, but in an ascending market, who cares? Right? Your asset was growing (usually). It was all just good times. And you reasonably derived that you could save money by doing it yourself. Now, when the economic sentiment and the euphoria have been whipsawed to heck and back, it's much easier to see that doing it yourself created a serious problem.

Just in case you're still in denial about the quality of help you were paying for before you started doing it yourself, here is a job listing from the Web site of one of Wall Street's biggest firms. The following are the job requirements for financial advisor/consultants, listed in their original order:

1. *Demonstrate ability to sell*
2. *Excellent problem solving, networking, communication, interpersonal and organizational skills*
3. *Interest in investments and financial markets*
4. *Demonstrate excellent work ethic and ability to multitask*

They then list experience requirements for potential advisors, again in following order:

1. *Prior sales experience*
2. *Prior business owner/entrepreneur*
3. *Prior professional service career*

Finally, they list the education requirements for potential advisors:

Bachelor's degree (Bachelors Degree not required for candidates with more than 5 years of sales experience)

Need I say more? Well maybe just a little. The truth is there was a very good reason, in a running bull market, that you came to believe you had just as many skills, if not more, than your financial advisor—because you most likely did.

A Coach for the Family Team

What do your tennis pro, your personal trainer, your yoga instructor, and your entourage of medical specialists all have in common (other than you owe them money)? They all want you to get better. Do you think your stockbroker wants you to get better? That's a good question, isn't it? Do you know how you can tell if your broker, advisor, or consultant really wants you to be a better investor/protector/financial sage and prudent risk manager as a Family Man? He will have told you so, and he will have done his best to guide you in that direction already.

Family Men Get It

Get good help. According to the Investment Company Institute, almost half of the 53.2 million American households (43.3 percent in 2014) own mutual funds, compared with only about 6 percent of households in 1980. With almost 8,000 mutual funds available today, you might need some help sorting it all out. Certainly, if your family's treasure chest is brimming with ducats and doubloons, you'll want better pricing and tax efficiency than mutual funds provide. If you've got more than $1,000,000 of investible assets, your use of mutual funds should be limited. The more money you have, the more you can demand greater efficiency in taxation strategies and fees. Besides, you undoubtedly can afford to hire the best money managers known to man because you're still riding around town in that convertible Cadillac I see you in every Sunday, so do it—get some help.

I saw the kiddy-seat in the back, no worries. Take my advice; get the best help you can afford.

Hire a trusted charioteer who does more than take you for a ride. You need someone who can keep your horses in line and keep you from rolling off a hillside. And while those are definitely important considerations, more importantly, you'll need someone who sees your family's aspirations the way you do, someone who knows whether you need basic investment solutions or more sophisticated wealth-management attention. You need someone who knows where you are in the evolution of your family's financial life cycle and what the needs of each of your stages are.

I look at it this way: if you going to have a successful charioteer, they've got to know all of the horses by name—their traits, their temperaments, their performance abilities, and most importantly, how to make them work together. Even more importantly, they need to know the dreams and plans of their clients and *always* be steering them toward financial security. Once you find that rare charioteer, then you and the little Spartans should be in good shape for generations to come. (It doesn't hurt if he also knows how to change a chariot tire from time to time.)

Here's a list of six basic criteria the Family Man can use when scouting for advisors. And when you're evaluating pitches, don't forget your radar speed gun. *Caveat emptor*: Let the buyer beware!

1. *What kind of training have they had, and can they prove it?*
   Ask to see their diplomas, certificates, and other evidence of formal education. Sometimes a lot of big words, a big fancy office, and on-the-job training are not enough. Sometimes people good at selling are not so good at getting the educational foundation your family needs. Ask to see their resume. Double-check it. If they get offended, walk out. If they're boasting phenomenally high returns, ask to see their audited statements. You can be polite about it, but when you get the statements, be sure you can double-check them.

2. *Check their U4 record online.*
   FINRA keeps a record of all the violations your advisor has racked up over the years. Check it out at www.finra.org. Type in their name and look under the section "Disclosure of Customer Disputes, Disciplinary, and Regulatory Events."

You'll be amazed. If they've got a bad mark, ask them to explain it. If they've got several, find the nearest exit, and thank goodness you checked.

They seemed like such nice people too…

3. *What is in it for them?*
Know how they are getting paid and how much they are getting paid. Are they fee only? Do they charge commissions? Do they charge by the hour? Which would be better for you? Are you going to be charged ongoing fees, such as 12-b1? Are there hidden fees? Have them estimate your annual costs in writing. Sometimes greater sophistication is worth a higher price. Sometimes a higher price is just a rip-off. In general, the higher your level of financial sophistication, the higher your advisor's level of knowledge will need to be. You will obviously pay more for greater expertise. Know your level and know what you need.

4. *What do you need and are they are they offering it?*
At what stage is your family in its financial life cycle? Do you need one-off investment products, investment management, financial planning, or all the above? Are they only offering you mutual funds and annuities? Can they handle your 144 restricted and control securities? Do you need private placement services or hedge-fund exposure? Do they have other resources they can refer to you—attorneys, accountants, auditors, and financial specialists?

5. *What is their standing in the community?*
Do other people you know use their services? What are they saying about them? Have they been a substantial benefit to

their clients? Have they served their community? Do they work in a charity you're familiar with? Are they active at a club, church, or school?

6. *Is it just more pie in the sky?*
Do they make you feel as if you're going to make a killing in the market? Are you as excited now as you were at the racetrack? Is your heart pounding furiously, your adrenalin rushing? Run, Bambi, run! If it seems too good to be true, then it's not true at all. The affluent Family Man needs someone with prudence, wisdom, and knowledge, not someone all jacked up in a bug-eyed "buy it!" "sell it!" 'roid rage.

No Whiny Kings

One of Alexander the Great's greatest generals was Ptolemy the Savior (cool name). He became the ruler of Egypt and founded the Ptolemaic Kingdom in 323 BC. But even after achieving so many great things in his life, having served valiantly under Alexander and becoming a ruler in his own right, Ptolemy was also a bit of a whiner. Like many a Family Man, he too neglected his studies. Once, while being tutored in mathematics by Euclid, the Father of Geometry, Ptolemy asked if there wasn't an easier way to learn this dreaded subject. Euclid's reply was swift and keen: "There is no royal road to geometry."

There is no royal road to anything you want as an achievement. You know that now. You've known it for a long, long time. Sacrifice, discipline, persistence, determination—these comprise the foundation of a Family Man's successes. There's a wonderful woman counting on you and no doubt a couple of ankle-biters looking up at you in awe and admiration. Do your work, men. The lives of your family and the families of your country are depending on it.

Pray

The prudent Family Man should pray and teach his kids to pray. Call upon the God of your family for clarity and wisdom. Even if you're not a believer, you and your family's spiritual preparations are still important. So do whatever you used to do to prepare your mind for a major challenge. What was your routine before a big game? What was your calming ritual before the hardest final exam of your educational career? How did you mentally prepare yourself for the test of your life? If you were ever in a life-threatening situation, do what you did then to steady your nerves now. That's how serious your financial preparation should be. Because buddy, this is a matter of life or death. Do those mental preparations as you plan the brilliant care of your family. Do them long before you make an investment decision. Ready yourself. Calm yourself. Set yourself for the great ride of life, because there will be some bone-jarring hits as well as some wonderfully thrilling ascensions.

I'm here to tell you that you will survive them all. Remember the pre-run routines of downhill skiers in the Winter Olympics? How they closed their eyes before the gate and rolled their heads, imagining every turn of the course, the speed they would run, the line they would take. Do that. Establish a pre-run routine that focuses all your attention, enhances your endurance, and calms your nerves. Make your plans wisely; know them by heart. Decide before a big market correction how you are going to react. Know where the economy is in its economic cycle. Manage your risk. Then get ready. Get all the angels on your side—the baby darlings at home and those in the highest heavens. Pray and work like Abraham Lincoln prayed and worked. It is said President Lincoln followed the admonition of St. Ignatius of Loyola and prayed as if everything depended upon God, but he worked as if everything depended only upon himself. C'mon men! You can do it!

Conclusion

There are hundreds if not thousands of voices out there barking the greatest stock market secrets known to humanity. Some of them are well-crafted hype-generators sure to pry every dollar from your piggy bank if you listen long enough. The important thing for Family Men to remember is to use your innate intelligence. When that's exhausted, borrow the brains of wise people around you. To invest well, you have to study, but study from the best, those who have made fortunes in the markets. Remember, there is no such thing as an easy buck, and a fast buck is an equally absurd belief. Money comes from WORK. You know that now. And you've got to do everything in your power—investment strategies, planning strategies, and protection strategies— to preserve your money and protect your wealth.

You're a Family Man! You don't need life to be easy or fast. You just need to be rewarded for your brilliant efforts and to keep those rewards for yourself, your wife and kids, and anyone else in the loving care of your family. But you've probably got work to do to get back on track. If this current economic confusion is any guide, you've probably got a fighting spirit to rekindle, finances to reorganize, trust to rebuild, and a lifetime of success to achieve. Remember the sacred mission you've chosen: to defend and protect, to teach and sustain your precious family.

If you're prepared for the worst you can imagine, then you will weather any downturn, any setback, any correction with dignity and purpose. Crisis is rife with disappointment, difficulty, and failure, but if you've organized good defenses, strategized against worst-case scenarios, and saved for that proverbial rainy day, your chances of survival will have greatly increased.

Remember too that you live in the United States of America. It is still the land of limitless opportunity. If that weren't true, there would be no night boats, no underground tunnels, no immigrant caravans clawing through the deserts to get here. People by the millions recognize what we've built, and they risk their lives to reach our shores each and every day. Don't give a second thought to anyone perched casually in comfortable opulence, academic or political, whose only rant is the single discord of despair toward our nation. Perhaps the people who can only find fault with the cultural successes of United States of America should join the next wave of desperate refugees huddled on our shores languishing for the hopeless evacuation out of the country to a better life of freedom and opportunity elsewhere. Oh wait... There aren't any!

On the other hand, don't allow yourself to get trapped by the witless assumption that American prosperity is up for grabs or that it arose with very little effort. Everything you see, every convenience you can't live without, was built with hard work, sweat, and perseverance—probably something your parents and grandparents had a lot to do with. Being financially fat and lazy is the perfect scenario for a financial heart attack. So stay lean. Stay fit. And take care of your family with your creator-endowed inalienable rights and American business know-how.

Now get your disciplines in order. Do the basics: Love your family. Take care of your family. Work. Insure. Save. Invest. Plan. Protect. Rinse and repeat. You'll be fine. Men, we've got a job to do. Let's get to it!

The Family Man's Stock Market Volatility Survival Guide Checklist

There is much for the Family Man to do to survive volatile stock markets. Use the following checklist as a quick reference:

Love your wife
Love your kids
Live for your family
Grow up
Curb your spending
Buy a Ferrari (just kidding)
Insure
Invest
Save
Live your life, not the neighbors'
Dream your goals
Plan
Protect the estate
Believe in our country, our economic culture, and our markets
Study
Resist TV
Grow corn in the beneficent universe
Work, work, work
Feed the beast

Go to asset classes

Diversify

Measure yourself

Balance and rebalance

Opportunism

Hire a pro

No whining

Pray (Probably should have put this first!)

Markets are volatile right now. The television news is only confusing things. Pundits are everywhere, contradicting themselves with every wild swing of the index. I'll say it one last time. Love your family. Take care of your family. Work. Insure. Save. Invest. Plan. Protect. You'll be fine.

If you see another Family Man who seems to be confused in these volatile markets, pass on this guide to him, but remember, this is *The Family Man's Stock Market Volatility Guide*. It was written for him and the benefit of his family *only*! I mean it! Male and female created he them. And God blessed them, and God said to them, Be fruitful, and multiply, and replenish the earth...

…Male and female created He them. And God blessed them, and God said to them, "Be fruitful, and multiply, and replenish the earth…" Genesis 1: 27-28

69503367R00071

Made in the USA
San Bernardino, CA
16 February 2018